Self
Deliverance

A Transformation of What You Were to What You Shall Be...
Beautiful Pain

Angelia Mitchell

CONTACT THE AUTHOR:
Angelia Lachelle Mitchell
20138 Spencer
Detroit, MI 48234
almenterprise50@yahoo.com
586-422-7884

Edited by Tenita Johnson
So It Is Written, LLC— SoItIsWritten.net
Editor does a disclaimer on the accuracy of all scripture.

Book Design by Shannon Crowley
Treasure Image & Publishing—TreasureImagePublishing.com

Dedication

This book is dedicated:

To my five beautiful children. Alicia Renea Mitchell, Anetra Trenea Franklin, Alexis Denea Drew, Totez D'Angelo Drew and Emanuel PeDale Robins.

To my four grandchildren Jaevun Lee Franklin, Patience Leah Franklin, Faith Lenea Franklin, and A'lurayh Lachelle Hand.

To my deceased parents. Herbert Lee Mitchell, Sr. and Patricia Ann Mitchell,

I would like to dedicate this book to everyone that pushed me and encouraged me in the time of preparation for the publication of this book.

I have to thank God, because it was He who inspired and gave me the idea and the title to pursue this book. I thank Him for the words that He whispered in my ear to help me create such a book. Writing this book saved my life. To God be the Glory for all that He has done!

Contents

Definitions

SELF: A person with essential being that distinguishes them from others, especially considered as the object of introspection or reflexive action. "Self" comes from the Old English, in which it means, "One's own person."

YOURSELF: Your sense of who you are, deep down—your identity. When you let someone else know you well, you reveal your true self to them. If the subject of your thoughts is you, you're thinking about yourself.

DELIVERANCE: The action of being reserved or set free; liberation, release, freeing, free.

Thou art my hiding place; Thou shalt preserve me
from trouble; Thou shalt compass me about with songs
of deliverance. Selah
"I will instruct thee and teach thee in the way which
thou shalt go; I will guide thee with Mine eye."
PSALM 32:7-8

The Spirit of the Lord is upon Me, because He hath
anointed Me to preach the Gospel to the poor. He hath
sent Me to heal the brokenhearted, to preach
deliverance to the captives, and recovering of sight to
the blind, to set at liberty them that are bruised.
ST. LUKE 4:18

Knowing Yourself

Oftentimes, we try to blame others for the way we act and for the decisions we make. Technically, it's you! The real problem is that we overlook ourselves. You must know and understand you. Be honest enough to recognize your own faults, problems, strengths and weaknesses. Understand your anger and your temperament—what pushes your buttons, what you hate, love, and what you're looking for in a mate.

It's important to know your level of tolerance when it comes to dealing with other people and situations. Understand what you can and can't take, what you're willing to deal with and what you can't deal with. Know your attributes, the things that has you bound, confused, stuck and discombobulated. You must know all these things about you! No one can do this for you. You must start putting things and your life into perspective because it will benefit your life.

Sometimes, it's best to be alone. Get to know yourself and allow God to mold you. Let Him show you, *you!* It took me a long time to realize that. Once I did, that's when I took ownership of myself. I saw myself in a different way. I didn't see myself the way people saw me. I saw myself the way God showed me about me. It was what He saw in me. Believe it or not, it made a difference in my life.

The love and the joy I have for others and my family was hidden in my heart. That love and joy needed to come out so I could fulfill my purpose and destiny. This was especially necessary for me to relate to different people, especially women. I call it, "My Breakout Moment." You, too, can have a "Breakout Moment." In this moment, you will see yourself in a different way—not the way people want to portray you, but in the way that God wants to *present* you.

God has a way of slowing you down and getting your attention. I had to look deep into my heart to see what I was doing as a woman and a mother. I had to focus on taking care of my family and doing the right thing for our lives, like having stability.

Stability became my primary focus. All my life, I made unwise choices. I "robbed Peter to pay Paul"; I was moving all the time instead of having a stable home which is essential to having a stable life. You're supposed to learn from your mistakes as you get older.

I made my life a little harder than normal by expecting everyone to understand me. Truthfully, I had to understand myself and what I was doing. I had to get to know *me*—my life and way of living, not the life of my parents. I had to find out which way my life was going to go. I prayed and remained in isolation until God revealed me to *me*.

God is our true anchor. He will teach us what to do and how to do it. God can show you and teach you anything you want to know—if you want to know it. If you have a misunderstanding about anything, He can show you that, too. God can teach us how to love the correct way from the heart. It is vital that we are led by God with our heart. Your heart says a lot about you, and how you are. You must learn to *know and love yourself first!* Doing this will keep you from trying to be something or someone that you're *not!* It's important.

In knowing yourself, you learn your true identity, your structure, your life, your likes and dislikes. You must become real and one with yourself, even when it hurts. (Note to Self: You're not going to like everything about *you*.)

All my life, I walked in the shadows of my parents. Out of three children, I was the only one who was birthed through my parents. That live what we saw and what we were taught. That's the reason why it's not good for children to see, hear or know certain things while they're young. They grow up with what they've seen, heard or know already planted in their minds. It's a seed that grows and ultimately becomes a part of their reality when they're adults.

I've always had a great work ethic. I love helping people, just like both of my parents. I'm more like my mother. She loved her family and wanted to keep everyone together, whether near or far. However, I realized I was living the life that my mom was dealt. I call it the "moving syndrome." Although my dad made all the money, he wasn't good at paying the bills. This hits home, too. I was just like my father in this area.

I was losing on every hand, all the way up into my forties. I couldn't go on living like this for the rest of my life. One day, God spoke to me. He said, *Self-Deliverance. I've given you the power to deliver yourself from the chains of bondage.* In other words, He said, "I've already delivered you! Now forgive and deliver yourself!" It may sound harsh, but it woke me up and it got my attention.

It may sound easy, but it wasn't. I didn't know what to do. I started fasting and praying, asking God to show me the next step and where to start. I thought saving all my money was it. Nope! It was about being a tither and a sower. Then one day, God blessed me to catch up on all my bills. He supplied all of my needs, without me saving, all while I was on short-term disability from work. What a God!

I guess you're wondering, how I delivered myself? I just started praising and worshipping God! In my car, at work, early in the mornings. No one knew. It was between me and God. That's when things started to shift and break in my life like no other. It's not when people get tired of you struggling and going through. It's when you start to understand and know *yourself!*

When you say, "Enough is enough," that's when you've gotten sick and tired of yourself. The battle is not yours; it belongs to God. God has a way and a better plan for you. You must adhere to the instructions that was given to you. You've missed time and time again because you thought you had it! I thought the same way. Knowing what I know now has made me a better person in business and ministry.

Deliverance is real. When you're delivered from yourself, that demon can't hold you down anymore! When you're delivered from yourself, you move to another level in God. Your life can change instantly if you allow yourself to go through the process of healing and deliverance.

The mirror is a true reflection of you and no one else. The mirror never lies. It's just shows you! You only see yourself. You may have to look in the mirror and ask yourself, Am I a self-made woman? Am I the woman God is molding? Am I true to myself? Am I true to people? You must be true and real with yourself. You matter! You should often find something new or old about yourself. Something that you just don't do anymore. Reflection is good, so take some time out to do so. God is the only one who truly knows you and your heart because He created you.

For I know the thoughts that I think toward you, saith the Lord, thoughts of peace and not of evil, to give you an expected end.
JEREMIAH 29:11

Remember, people come into your life for a reason, a season or a lifetime. God is there, no matter what! He knows all about them. He wants you to know where to place them. I tell you getting to know yourself is worth it. Knowing yourself is beneficial. It helped me heal from the inside out. Go ahead and get to know you! You'll be surprised at what you'll find. Become the greatest you that you know that you can be! You owe it to yourself.

Self

SELF: *A person's essential being that distinguishes them from others, especially considered as the object of introspection or reflexive action.*

One should know about self, know what you are made of. What you were created for. Self is a word all on its own. It best describes you. *No one else!* It defines who you are. Self is all about you shaping and forming your*self*. Taking your*self* the distance, knowing what it takes to succeed. Self, don't quit! Self, don't give up! Self, persevere! Self, pray and push! Self, be strong and have self-discipline. Obstacles will come; position your*self* to get a good running start to leap over that hurdle. When you look in the mirror, it's just you staring back at you. Everything you are and everything you desire to be is in the hands of God and yourself.

Trust and believe in all that you do. There can never be another *you!*

Repeated Cycles

1) **REPEAT**: Something that you do or say over and over again.

2) **CYCLES**: A series of events which are regularly repeated in the same order.

3) **REPEATED CYCLES**: Doing (1) and (2) constantly. They could have been brought on by a generational curse or from a lineage, or by your own habits that will start a new curse in your bloodline. This cycle is relevant in today's world.

When you've been doing the same exact thing more than once, that's not a circle; it has become a cycle. It happened to me. I thought maybe it was the way of life. But once you dig deeper, God starts to reveal things to you.

Mine started as a generational curse. It started with my parents. When I was a child, all we did was move. I thought that was normal. No! That was not normal; that was instability. Although I was in church, I couldn't understand what was happening in my life. Generational curses attach to you like clothes. It takes God to deliver you from it. You first have to recognize it and call that thing out! Let the devil know that you have identified it.

I've been homeless, jobless, financially unstable and unable to pay bills. I've moved constantly, been without transportation, rode the bus and have lived in hotels until houses were available while raising five children. But through it all, God allowed me to keep my family together. Even now!

When a repeated cycle constantly recurs, it means that you haven't learned the lesson, or you may be unaware of what's going on. Either way it's a problem. You must be willing to fight to do what is right! It's a must because if you don't deal with it, it can ruin your life, your credit, your business and friendships. How can you establish a business if you're constantly going in cycles?

There is still some breaking off that God has to do for me, so you are not alone! I want to be totally free from repeated cycles. You must put things in order and prioritize your life. I've come to realize that I was dealing with a *repeated cycle* in my life—not even knowing that it was a generational curse. Once I acknowledged it, I was still repeating the cycle! I actually had to acknowledge that I needed help. I needed to be delivered from *me!* I needed deliverance from all the bad decisions that I was making. I realized that I didn't need help from people; I needed help from God.

A repeated cycle is a form of disobedience when you refuse to listen to God. God speaks to us through the Holy Spirit to warn us and keep us from danger. God speaks to us all. You must know His voice. If you don't know His voice, how would you know who's speaking to you? God's voice speaks truth! He wants you to obey. When you're thinking about doing something wrong, He whispers, *do the right thing.* It's God's way of giving you directions. If you don't heed the warning, you will suffer the consequences of your decisions. Heeding the voice of God is how you stay out of trouble.

Repeated cycles are cycles you don't want to stay in. It keeps you in a terrifying state. It's bad when you get so used to repeating cycles that you believe it's normal. The sad part about it is, you're already used to it and you're comfortable in it. It's your way of living; but the reality is that you're dying.

This is a cycle that you must conquer with God's help! Cycles of any kind will leave scars on you and your family. What are your cycles? These cycles can be broken. I encourage you to pray and fast. Fight through this journey of your last experience with your repeated cycle. God's plan is better and more phenomenal than yours.

Say this with me: "I will not repeat another cycle!"

Fight!

You have to *fight!* Fight for your *deliverance!* It all belongs to *you!*

You must fight! Fight like never before. You still have enough fight left in you for another round; fight the good fight of faith. Fight for your children, fight for your marriage, fight for your loved ones, fight for your freedom.

Fight for your life, fight for your future.

Fight! Fight! Fight!

You deserve better, you deserve to live free. You deserve to love and be loved.

Fight with every beat of your heart, fight with strength! Fight for your health, fight for your healing, fight for success, fight to end all generational curses in your family. Fight for wisdom, fight for your family, fight for your ministry, fight for your mantels.

Fight! Fight! Fight!

GOD+FIGHT+DELIVERANCE = FREE

Rejection

REJECTION: Broadly defined, social rejection refers to social rejection; rejection of social acceptance, group, inclusion or belonging. Rejection comes in a variety of forms and content. Relationships, friendships, friends, family and groups. Rejection produces negative effects and can lead to antisocial behavior depending on interaction. Rejection is painful to the individual who has to deal with any form of *rejection*.

I've had the privilege of being rejected and it wasn't a pleasant feeling. I realized throughout my life that I held rejection in my heart towards the ones who rejected me and my family. Rejection hits hard, especially when it's from people you call family or friends. Coming from a world of rejection, you don't want to be bothered with anyone because you don't want to be hurt again.

I'll never forget the time I dropped my mom off at a relative's house. My mom was blind at the time. As we walked into their home, she told me to have Mom sit in the den, while everyone else was up front in the dining room talking and eating. I left my mom in their care. Oh! Did I mention that it was Thanksgiving? I kissed my mom and told her that I'll be back. I was gone for a couple of hours. When I returned to pick her up, I found her still sitting in the same spot where I left her. I felt like they rejected my mom. My mom expressed to me how badly her feelings were hurt!

They forgot about my mom. When she told me how she felt, I couldn't believe it! I felt her pain! How could they laugh, joke, eat and forget that she was even in the house? She was there for hours, and no one realized that she was even in the back room. My mom never wanted to go to another family gathering again. Even when someone that's close to you like your parents get rejected or looked over, it hurts!

Rejection will always be a part of life. You must know how to handle it, or it will handle you. You'll experience rejection from a job, church, leaders, people, business, loved ones, family, friends, and relationships. You must be careful *not* to reject others. Being hurt and rejected can cause you to also hurt others out of your pain. Learning how to overcome the misery of rejection means acknowledging that there is an issue.

Oftentimes, when we're rejected, we tend to look at ourselves differently. Sometimes, it's not about us being rejected. Most of the times it's the one who's doing the rejecting. They've been hurt by rejection, too. Rejection is a ball of pain that people use when they've been mistreated or hurt. It becomes their wall of defense.

Rejection often causes one to act in such a way that they do not feel wanted, loved, accepted or worthy. We must understand the bigger plan behind rejection. Rejection is a part of life to mature us. It is also God's way of strengthening and preparing us for ministry so we can help others who suffered from rejection.

Another beautiful part of rejection is that God uses it as a form of protection. Oftentimes, rejection is God's way of protecting you from something that could change the course of your life. Rejection possibly prevented death. Satan's job is to distract you with the pain of rejection. You may not understand everything, but God does. It's vital for us to trust God with our whole heart.

Now that you understand that rejection is good and a form of God's protection, I'm sure now you'll have a greater appreciation for it. God truly knows what's best for each of us. We choose to alter situations to fit our lives and not His plans. Oftentimes, we ask questions like, "Why do certain things have to be a part of our life? Like being rejected?" It's not for you to be defeated; it's for you to pass the test so you can go to the next level in ministry, as well as in life.

People come into our lives for a reason, a season or for a lifetime. A *reason* means that person is there to teacher you something. A *season* is just for a limited time, but it's still for a purpose. A *lifetime* would be like a marriage joining two together as one. That's the reason for it all. Rejection is to teach us and limit us for a purpose. It's not about who's giving the lesson; the question is, *are you learning from the lesson?*

I understand why this book, *Self-Deliverance* was meant for me to write. It was strengthening me to know that my shortcomings are my victory and a tool to help others through my life testimony. Rejection is necessary! Now I understand that rejection is not the end of my life. But it was the making of my life, and it will be the making of yours.

Acceptance

ACCEPTANCE: *The action or process of being received as adequate or suitable. Typically to be admitted into a group.*

Acceptance is what we look for from people, and not God, no matter who they are or what their social status is. We do all that we can to fit in, to be a part, to be mentioned, seen and loved by a group of people. We want acceptance in our relationships, dating, work, and ministry. We do all of this to feel or be accepted instead of us being ourselves. We all want to be accepted and wanted. But, to what degree?

We give our all and make changes just to fit in. We will even go to the lengths of rejecting someone else to be accepted—whether it be friendships, a relationship or business, just to be a part of a click or inner circle. *Just as long we're in* becomes the goal!

Acceptance often comes with a lot, like attachments, manipulation, downplaying, lying, and being fake. All of these things ultimately lead to misery. It's like "keeping up with the Joneses," and yet, you still have nothing.

Acceptance is a job. You must work at it and dress a certain way. You must fake like you got it all just to be accepted. However, all you need is God! His acceptance of you is different. God accepts you whole, even with all of your faults, flaws, imperfections and lies. Yes! God accepts it all because He knows you and He's the only one who can change you. It's okay to be accepted in some things in life; it's called being appreciated.

Man's acceptance always comes with a cost; God's acceptance doesn't. It only costs us when we neglect to do what we're supposed to do. It costs us when we don't accept God's plan or will for our lives. When we accept the world's acceptance, we're accepting Satan's world—the good, the bad, and the ugly.

We must learn to accept ourselves for who we are. You must know you—the things you like, what makes you happy and what it's going to take to get you where you need to be. Acceptance is good if the acceptance will help push you.

You should know if the people around you are true. There's no harm in asking why a person is accepted. Are you being accepted for popularity? Is it to meet a goal or is it genuine? When people generally accept you, it's for a reason. Therefore, be careful of the circles and the cliques you cling to—where people can come in and minimize you because of acceptance.

Learn to be you! There's no right or wrong to being you. You were born in this world alone and you will leave this world alone. We spend too much time trying to figure out why people don't like us. Naturally, we must accept ourselves. We have to create what we want; but in the creating, we must believe in the Creator. God created us for His plan and His purpose. God accepts you for you. Now accept yourself.

God is simply saying, "I need your acceptance. Accept me?" God will and can be all that you need Him to be. The only person you need acceptance from is God and God Alone.

Ask yourself this: "How much does acceptance cost?" You add it up. Will it be worth it in the end or can you live without being "accepted"?

ACCEPTANCE

Acceptance will always be a part of life. We must

Choose to accept or decline it. The

Choice is yours. We all have a journey that we must take in order for us to reach our destiny depending on what we choose.

Everyone is not exempt from it.

Pray and ask God to lead you.

Trust that God will do

A new thing to you and through you. You're

Never alone; accept

Christ today and receive

Everlasting life and acceptance.

It's a Part of the Process

Everything you've had to go through, and everything you've came out of, was all a part of the process. Your process is unique to you and is not like anyone else. Your process is *your* process, and it's required for your life.

> *The steps of a good man are ordered by the Lord, and*
> *He delighteth in his way.*
> PSALM 37:23

Just because we plan, build and have a blueprint for our own life doesn't mean that it is God's blueprint for our lives. Therefore, it's so important to consult God every day concerning our lives and our decisions. God has the master plan, and we should want our steps to be ordered by Him.

We win more in life then we think. Connecting with the Connector allows us to have victory. It's like playing chess.

You must be patient, strategize and study your opponent while waiting for the perfect move to declare checkmate! It's the same with God. We must stay focused on God and be ready when the right opportunity presents itself. God's timing is always on time.

> *... The race is not to the swift,*
> *nor the battle to the strong ...*
> ECCLESIASTES 9:11

There is a series of steps that need to be taken to achieve your desired success. Those steps are part of the process. You may be in your process season right now! Some may be starting their process. Others may be in the middle of their process while others are exiting the process, which simply means BREAKTHROUGH! The process will not be pretty. The process is to position you. It will feel uncomfortable, scary, and crazy.

You may not understand or comprehend anything that's happening. You may experience rejection during the process. You may hear people talking about you; you may lose things, friends, family, home, car or job during the process. Eventually, you'll find yourself in the middle of your process, and it will all start to make sense. God will start to reveal things and line things up for you.

Your faith in God gets stronger as you become stable. God makes ways out of no way for you. He'll give you favor, rearrange the problems and situations in your life.

If you're at the end of the process, you're shifting into your destiny. Everything is now aligned. Your prayer life has changed, people have changed, and your circle has changed. God has put influential people in your life who see your growth and your gift. They're there to help you get to your destiny. It was all a part of the process.

GOD+YOU+PROCESS = BREAKTHROUGH

Chapter Six

Emotions

EMOTION: A natural instinct of state of mind deriving from one's circumstances, mood, or relationships with others. Instinctive or intuitive feeling as distinguished from reasoning or knowledge.

Emotions! Emotions! Emotions! Yes, we all have them. Emotions tell your heart and mind what to do, how to feel and express itself. But we must learn how to control them, and not let them control us. Our emotions will have us feeling all kinds of ways if we allow them to. Men's and women's emotions are all the way different. Women tend to wear their emotions on both sleeves. Most men tend to hide their emotions and are good at doing so. However, there are some who are more expressive and don't mind sharing how they're feeling. Even though we are all born with emotions, we just choose to deal with them differently.

Women are naturally emotional. We are loving and nurturing. We are concerned with the way we look and feel.

Emotions play a part in how we act, the way we respond to others, talk to one another, what we wear, and our body language. Our hormones are also responsible for our emotions. Our emotions can be seen on our faces and in our eyes.

Women, our emotions are like riding a roller coaster. Our emotions carry us up and down, and in and out of our feelings, saying and imagining things that we shouldn't.

Our emotions will have us going in circles, taking sharp turns and dips and hitting corners. Right when we think it's over, we're hit by another high, steep drop. Then it starts to level out.

A good man out of the good treasure of his heart bringeth forth that which is good; and an evil man out of the evil treasure of his heart bringeth forth that which is evil; for of the abundance of his heart his mouth speaketh.
LUKE 6:45

We must know how to control our emotions. It is not easy at all. Therefore, we need help from God. He is the only one who can help us mature in this area. We must understand what we are doing when it comes to handling our emotions. We can get all worked up and discombobulated! We may start throwing things around, talking and spreading accusations, lying, spreading rumors, gossiping all because of our emotions. Sometimes, men and women start cheating all because of uncontrolled emotions.

Good communication is the key. We must learn how to effectively communicate, no matter what it is about or who it is with. Emotions can be determined in so many ways and factors. Emotions can be loving and brutal at the same time. Emotions can be felt at an early age. Emotions can be developed in different scales dependent on a person's mental state.

Emotions can show you a person's feeling towards you or humanity, whether it's good or bad. Emotions can have you going from being the nicest person in the world to being the meanest person around. They can also have you seeing a psychiatrist. Emotions can have you in and out of love, seeing red and ready to kill or hurt someone. Your feelings can have you isolated from one another with no social life or without any friends. Emotions can be an outward sign of what's hiding inside.

Yes! Your emotions can get the best of you—if they're not controlled! God created us and He is the only one who knows what it will take to heal us and help us to manage our emotions. We must get to the heart of the matter before our emotions take control of our lives. God is the only one who can help us in this area.

A Prayer for Emotions

Heavenly Father, thank you for this day. Lord, I come to you as humble as I know how, asking you for forgiveness. Forgive me of my many sins, sins known and unknown.

I come asking you for help! Help heal me from my emotions. God, help me to place my emotions in their rightful place in my life. I ask that you help me to love, to be patient with others. You said in your word to love our neighbors as we love ourselves. God, teach me and train me how to implement emotions in my life daily.

Teach me how to control my emotions when they start to arise. God, I ask that you put them under my feet.

Oh God! From this day forth, teach me how to be accountable for my emotions. Oh God, in the name of Jesus, I look to you for help! God, help me!

God, help me even in my situations. Most of all, Lord, give me to control when I speak or how I react.

Lord, I give it to you, and I lay it at your feet. In the name of Jesus, I do pray.

Thank God. Amen!

Come Out the Box

BOX: *A container with a flat base and sides, typically square or rectangular, made of wood, metal, cardboard and often with a lid or removable cover. A case, receptacle.*

What is your box? How tight is your box? Is it full? Remember, it has a removable cover or lid.

Coming out of the box is not an easy thing to do. You must have courage. Once you've placed yourself there, it's hard to come out! You might be saying, "How can someone be placed in a box?" It's simple. By allowing people to put, push or place you there. People know exactly what they've done to place you and to keep you there. I call it the trap. Sometimes you may not know that you're even in a box until you have flipped your lid.

Some people will never know that they're trapped in a box until something major happens. Something like people tearing down your name, calling you cold as ice, dead battery, negative. Saying things like, "no one wants to be around you, you're killing the vibe." And you wonder why people are saying these things about you. Could it be a misconception or feeling that someone has about you? But they got that from someone else.

You try to ignore it, overlook it, let it pass, pretend like it never happened or is happening. However, it must be addressed. It starts to feel and look like the big elephant in the room has sat on your box with you in it. You keep pushing the top or the lid open so that you can address it and that's when you realize that the elephant is actually sitting on your box. With no more strength to push, you're trapped in your own box with your lid closed tight.

You've tried over and over to get out of the box. To socialize and mingle with the others. To become a part of the environment or Society. They just won't let you out! I came to realize, after being in the box, that I had time to seek God. I asked God what was wrong with me. Was it me or was it them? I couldn't understand the mistreatment or their concept about me. Then one day I heard God say to me, "It's not you. It's them." All I could do was cry.

God told me that it was the people. Remember God will always confirm His word. It just simply means that there's something about you that they have a problem with. Instead of addressing the problem with you, they choose to get a clique, or as I call it, "The Amen section." Others that may agree or feel the same way about you and others. People love to try and feel superior over you until it happens to them. All they have to do is get to know you.

> *Moreover, if thy brother shall trespass against thee, go and tell him his fault between thee and him alone. If he shall hear thee, thou hast gained thy brother. But if he will not hear thee, then take with thee one or two more, that "in the mouth of two or three witnesses every word may be established." And if he shall neglect to hear them, tell it unto the church; but if he neglect to hear the church, let him be unto thee as a heathen man and a publican.*
> MATTHEW 18:15-17

The lies people have told, heard, fabricated, fueled, or felt condone what your haters think about you. Until one day you yell and scream so loud, and cry so hard that only God heard you.

Then He set up His master plan to expose it all. He allowed the ones (that you allowed to place you in the box) to be there. He did this so that they could hear and acknowledge the truth, and you could display your heart in front of your haters. God will allow one person to feel the pain of your heart and defend you.

God knows the fakers, haters and pretenders. From the ones that truly have a genuine heart towards you, God will show you that the box that you're in is suffocating you, but it is making you. God will allow you to leave them and not him. God will vindicate you. You can't fool God.

Say this with me out loud: "Come out the box!"

God couldn't use me in my brokenness. This was His way of preparing me for my breakthrough.

Many of you may feel like you're in a box, but I command over your life right now! I command you to come out that box! I command a push like no other, to help you push the lid or whatever maybe sitting on your box to open or explode! In the name of Jesus! Take dominion this day! Do not let anyone place or put you in a box and sit on it again! Prepare for your breakthrough and healing. Come out the box!

A box is a way that Satan tries to keep you down, in bondage, discouraged, inactive and bound. But God is the box opener even when they're sitting on it. Catch this! God is stronger than the object, person or thing sitting on the box. Make this your declaration this day! Say this out loud as you read it.

My Declaration!

I declare and decree that this box will not house
or hold me again!

I declare and decree that I will no longer let
people place me back in a box!

I declare and I decree that I will never let
anyone sit on my box again!

What God has placed in me is bigger than any box. I will stand up, and out of this box. Declaring my total victory! Never to let anyone sit on me. What I thought was making me weak has made me strong! God is my vindicator, and He has vindicated me!

To Satan! Hear me roar!!! You thought you had me sealed in a box. My God has other plans for me. God came and ripped the top off the box and out came a winner fighting, stronger than before!

My Declaration!

Never ever will I be placed or sealed in a box.

GOD+YOUR BOX = DESTROYED

Deliver Yourself from You: Forgive You

FORGIVE: *Stop feeling angry or resentful toward (someone) for an offense, flaw, mistake.*

One thing's for sure, we don't like to believe who we are, what we've become or what we like to do.

In the first chapter, we discussed knowing yourself. You must know and understand yourself—including the good, the bad and the ugly. Whatever happened in your past is just what it is. Your past. It will only prevent you from moving forward to your future if you allow it to do so. Leave the past in the past, forgive yourself and move on.

Many people don't know how to forgive themselves. I was one of those people. It was hard. I didn't understand why I had to do it. However, I learned that it was necessary. Forgiving myself helped me to free myself *from me.*

God wants you to forgive yourself, as we forgive others. It's not a crime to forgive you. It's a form of release. After I forgave myself, I asked God to forgive me and all of my foolishness. So, forgive yourself so that you can move on. You hold yourself hostage when you don't deal with your own issues. Oftentimes, you want everyone else to forgive you and the truth is that you matter, too. You should matter to *you*. Once you learn how to forgive yourself, then you'll be able to see things differently.

Deliverance is a process for everyone. It's like shedding old skin to make room for new skin to develop, but this time you will not be covered by skin, but by God. Free yourself by forgiving yourself. Forgive yourself for being in that abusive relationship or marriage, for that decision to "rob Peter to pay Paul," for failing to meet that goal or start that business. Forgive *you!*

Forgive yourself and free yourself from the misery of those bad thoughts, temptations, suicidal thoughts and notions. God wants you to be free and free indeed. He wants you to explore a new life of expectation! A new life knowing that nothing can keep you or hold you in bondage anymore! A new life with God.

God knows more about you than you think He does. God has a plan for your life. *"For I know the thoughts that I think towards you, saith the Lord, thoughts of peace, and not of evil, to give you an expected end"* (JEREMIAH 29:11). In order to move forward into the things God has planned for you, you must forgive yourself. And after you have forgiven yourself, ask God to forgive you for not forgiving yourself.

Abba Father

Abba Father, it's me, (insert your name). I come to you as humble as I know how, asking you, Father, to forgive me of my many sins, known and unknown.

Lord, I need you! I need your help! Help me to understand me! Lord, I ask that you help me to forgive myself of things that I allowed to control me and that were out of my control.

I need to forgive myself for things, decisions, people, ways that I have taken, that has made it hard for me and my family. Lord, help me to make the right decisions for my life and family. I forgive myself from this moment on. No more looking back, only forward.

I forgive myself. From my heart, my spirit and my soul. Now rejoice! Hallelujah!

Greater is coming!

DELIVER YOURSELF FROM YOU=FORGIVE YOU

Forgive yourself for the things that you can't change. Forgive yourself for the things that you have lost, whether it was by your own hands or someone else's. Forgive yourself, for it's time to move on. Never look back! Forgive yourself for the ten thousandth time! For the last time!

Forgive yourself for failing your family over and over again.

Forgive yourself for the millions of times *you* said that you would never do it again or let that happen. Forgive yourself for losing control and blaming everyone else. Forgive yourself for not taking responsibility of your life and future.

Forgive! For you are forgiven.

If we confess our sins, He is faithful and just to forgive us our sins, and to cleanse us from all unrighteousness.
1 JOHN 1:9

Judge not, and ye shall not be judged. Condemn not, and ye shall not be condemned. Forgive, and ye shall be forgiven.

LUKE 6:37

Healed

HEAL: (Past tense: healed) to make healthy, whole, or sound, restore to health, free from ailment; to bring to an end or conclusion, as conflict between people or groups usually with the strong implication of restoring former amenity; settle, reconcile; They tried to heal the rift between them but were unsuccessful.

Oh! What a feeling to be healed! To have your heart and your natural feelings back. To never look back to what was. Look forward to the future. Self-deliverance heals every area of your life—your heart, mind, body, spirit and soul. Your scars and brokenness. The two main organs that work together are the heart and the mind. Because they work as one, when both are damaged, they work against each other.

God never intended for you to be incomplete. God needs us to be whole. Your breakthrough requires for you to be made whole. You need to be healed and made whole for the next person or relationship—even for your next assignment and your marriage. You must be made whole and ready to serve. God heals every place that is broken, hurt or hidden. All you have to do is recognize it and acknowledge it. Pray and acknowledge it to God. He's the ultimate healer of your soul.

He wants you healed from yourself—your emotions, the way you think, speak, react. He wants to heal those years filled with hurt, pain and scars. God wants to heal all of those things that you've been hiding in the crevices of your soul and in the back of your mind. These are the things we don't want to acknowledge or deal with, but God does. Let Him heal you because a healed person is a better person. A healed person is an unstoppable person who's ready to take on the world.

The healing process is the start of something big in your life. Get ready for the best years of your life. You will never be the same. You owe it to yourself to be completely healed. That's a lot of years to be carrying all that weight!

We are all hurting from something or someone. We can't let it take over our lives. You must get in control of your pain and learn how to release it. Your life will never be as it was because it's always changing for the better. People who are healed can relate to others and their pain, and effectively minister to them. Healing is available to all who want to be healed. Allow God to restore you back to having a healthy life. Change is good! It also shows maturity. Look in the mirror and introduce yourself to the healed you!

HEALED

Healed, is what you need to be in order for you to

Experience a restored life. It's time that we have an encounter with God the

Almighty, loving the new you in

Life that you are living, and that God is creating for you.

Every passion of your life is being merged back to its rightful effect so that you may make an impact in someone else's life. And tell your testimony of your

Deliverance!

You are healed!

Deliverance from It All

Wow! What a feeling to know that all the things that you've been through has brought you to this point of deliverance. To be free from it all and begin a new life. You just overcame those problems that have been plaguing your life for years, stopping you from growing as an individual, in your family, in your ministry, in your business, your goals, dreams and leadership commitment.

If you had embraced deliverance a long time ago, can you imagine how far you would have been right now? But God! God knew what it was going to take for you to walk into your own deliverance. Deliverance is for everyone. God delivers those who know they need a change in their lives. They know that they've been called. But they've been running for a long time and running from the assignment of their ministry that God has called them to. What a feeling to know that God can deliver you and restore you. God loves you that much.

For God so loved the world, that he gave his only begotten Son, that whosoever believeth in him should not perish, but have everlasting life.
JOHN 3:16

All that you've been through had to happen—the good, the bad and the ugly. Think about it. If you hadn't gone through it, you wouldn't be free to become all that God has called and predestined you to be. Nothing in your life happens by happenstance. Everything has been ordained by God. Although we chose to take a different path, God still had us covered.

God is forever trying to get us on the right path of His plan. When we learn to accept God's help and deliverance, we'll see and feel things differently. God will open our eyes to see and know that this is the right path to take. Just follow His instructions.

The Bible tells us in 2 Corinthians 5:7, "*For we walk by faith and not by sight.*" That's exactly what it means. No matter what it looks like in front of you, your faith can conquer what you can't see. It helps our faith to grow and mature.

Deliverance is so vital to your life. You must believe that God is truly a deliverer. He's able to deliver you from situations that've been hidden and hunting you for so many years. These voids, problems, and issues have been buried deep down in the crevices of your soul. God knows it's there. If you'll allow Him to deliver you and bring you out, you can walk in the newness of life. God didn't bring you this far to leave you. God wants you to pray, pursue and press. He wants you to conquer, believe, have faith and grow.

I say this all the time: Holiness is right for me. Deliverance is crucial for living in true holiness. Also, developing and building a relationship with God is vital. When I say a relationship, I mean intimacy. You must be intimate with God. Intimacy with God means having personal, one-on-one time in His presence. This is the place where He can enter in and deal with the inner you. This is crucial to the process of deliverance. Deliverance is to restore you.

I've spent half my life fighting a generational curse. My deliverance came from fasting and praying, and from having my Pastor and First Lady lay hands on me, and pray for me.

I had to learn how to be humble. I had to understand myself. I got tired of fighting me! I was the primary cause of my own hang-ups and repeated cycles.

God had already delivered me; I had to deliver myself. I was the one going back, picking up the pieces and starting it all over again. I call it the perfect detox for my soul. I detoxed from all the things that I placed in my body, mind and in my heart. You can detox too. Allow God to remove all the impurities in your body, even the things that *you* placed there.

Sin and disobedience make you feel and look old. Deliverance revitalizes the body! Deliverance gives you strength, durability, love, freedom and courage. It allows you to live again in the fullness of life, the way that you were intended to live. The choice is yours. I declare and I decree that you will not go back to the old you.

A spiritual detoxification is one of the best detoxes you can have. It's a cleansing for the entire body and soul. Deliverance is available to you now—to be delivered from anything that you can think of or imagine. You can be free to become the best *you* that you can possibly be.

As you look back over your life, you will see that God was with you every step of the way. You didn't lose your way. You were distracted. I asked you to pray that God will remove every distraction, every friend who's not your friend, every enemy that's before you, every snake that's slithering around you. I asked God to just remove them right now in the name of Jesus!

Stretch out in God and be all that He has called you to be. I encourage you, my brother and my sister, to seek God's face and not His hand. Believe in His everlasting power. Know that He can deliver you from anything. We serve a possible God who makes all things new. Go ahead and seek God for your deliverance; it's free to all.

Now you can look to the future, knowing that nothing is holding you back and keeping you in bondage. You're free from it all! Now, be free to expand in love, to seek and to feel things. Start the process to every project God has deposited in you. You were built for this. Go ahead and say it out loud, "I'm free from it all! I'm free!"

No one and nothing can place you back in bondage. You are free from all burdens, lies, brokenness, disappointment, defeat, low self-esteem, loneliness, guilt and shame. You've been delivered from it all—your mind, your body, your spirit and soul. God has shifted you right into position, into your next level of possibilities and blessing.

God has delivered me from many things my mind couldn't even fathom. God made me realize that I had gotten this far with Him. He has delivered me and He's delivering you right now! God is giving you the power, the wisdom and the knowledge to understand. How to help yourself stay delivered. As you read this book, get ready for the ultimate to happen in your life. Things that you never thought would be, will be! You have been positioned. You've been delivered from it all for His purpose.

If anyone ask you what happened to you? Just tell them, God did it! He delivered you from it all!

Meet the Author

Mother of five children who's blessed with the gift of writing, Angelia Mitchell is the author of *Single with God's Benefits* and *Deliverance of The Mind*. She's the CEO of Glorified Production, founder of Woman2Woman, "Can We Talk" Ministry. Her mission is to uplift, encourage and motivate women of all colors.

Created by God and inspired by the Holy Spirit, *Self-Deliverance* serves as a reminder that God is real, and we are intended to live a guilt-free life.

www.ingramcontent.com/pod-product-compliance
Lightning Source LLC
Chambersburg PA
CBHW070319160726
47999CB00003B/1081